BLYTHE EDWARDS

Balancing Your Bipolar

This book was professionally typeset on Reedsy.
Find out more at reedsy.com

Contents

Testimonials

My conversation with Blythe was very eye-opening. She was able to validate some of the thoughts and feelings I was having as a parent of a bipolar child. More importantly, she was able to explain how she managed her highs, so that when her lows hit, they weren't as devastating. I was finally able to understand how to help my daughter manage her highs and advocate for her increased need for sleep during her lows. I was able to realize that sleeping was a normal requirement for proper healing of her body, from overdoing it when she was manic. This stopped the nagging and allowed me to support her and encourage the healing.

—Stacy

When I called Blythe, I immediately felt validated in the confusion and frustration I felt when it came to opening up about my illness. Very few times in my life had I shared my diagnosis with close friends and family, but with such a recent diagnosis I had not known how to inform an employer. Talking to Blythe helped me learn to describe my working abilities according to my strengths, then clarifying certain limitations based on my illness. This way, my employer understood how Bipolar was defined according to MY life rather than that of a textbook or other prior experience. Giving enough appropriate information helped me feel in control and confident, rather than allowing my employer to jump to conclusions.

—Kiana

Introduction

Finding balance in mental health is a lifelong challenge. This is even more clear when you have "bipolar." The very word brings to mind a sense of dissonance and imbalance.

It doesn't have to be that way. In my journey I have discovered a better way to find balance in bipolar. I have designed this book to share my story and help guide you to your own version of a well-balanced life.

This book is for anyone struggling to find that balance in their life. I hope it will make you laugh and cry, and in the end, will move you to be empowered to start your journey to find balance.

I am a young mom who has been working to find balance for 12 years. I have shared my techniques with many others over that span of time.

Many people have already found great success by implementing the techniques I will walk you through in the last chapters.

My life is an example of how well these techniques have worked together to improve my family's and my life. These past two years have been such a stark contrast to the years before. I have an incredible life. We have everything we need, and are working to improve every day.

I have so much freedom with my time. Heck, I got to go to the zoo with my girls and my mom all day long at one day's notice! I have three gorgeous baby girls. I have the best husband, who is creative and funny and loves me; bipolar and all.

I have two huge families, my husband's and mine, most of whom live within 30 minutes of me and are so supportive. We could have a bit less stress, but we are working, just like you, with the steps you will find as you read on, to manage and take things one day at a time.

We purposely work from home so that my husband and I can parent together and fully utilize our different strengths to care for each other and our girls. This is a sacrifice, but it has been worthwhile.

I promise, as you work hard with the steps in the second half of this book, and experiment with them; you will see a difference! I'm not saying you will be cured, as I believe bipolar is an ongoing battle, but you can improve and find greater balance as you implement more of these techniques.

Keep doing what you have already found to be helpful in managing your life.

Keep doing what you have already found to be helpful in managing your life. By adding in one new strategy at a time, I have found significant improvements in my symptoms and capacity.

I hope you can relate to my story and find comfort in knowing you aren't alone. I hope you can take away a few of the tips and tools to help you on your journey to creating your own version of normal!

I

Memoir

1

I'm Not Normal

Finding out at 17 that I have bipolar, isn't the way a typical teenager wants to end their senior year. What I thought were normal teenage issues were now categorized as abnormal.

But all I heard was *"You're not normal."*

Teenagers already feel out of place. Having it confirmed is pretty devastating.

In February 2008, four weeks after having my wisdom teeth removed, and being on a pain killer I reacted poorly to, I went to see a psychiatrist. This doctor happened to be the same one who had missed the bipolar diagnosis three years earlier, even though my dad had been there to verify my mood swings. It is common to miss the diagnosis during hypomania, but this doctor didn't seem to ask much about me before writing off my behavior as "typical".

When a bipolar individual sees a psychiatrist, they need to bring a close family member or friend who can describe their moods. This is because of an interesting phenomenon: When we are depressed, it is extremely hard to remember the good times. Our brains seem to store the memories and emotions in the same place. When we are happy, it is hard to recall the depression. When I'm feeling good, it is hard for me to remember that some days I don't even want to leave the house.

If a person who has bipolar is seen in their depression, they are often diagnosed with unipolar depression. This diagnosis is most common because the depressed state is when bipolar individuals are willing to seek help. Missing the diagnosis is especially dangerous because many antidepressants when used alone, can induce hypomania or mania.

I did not like my psychiatrist. She threatened to send me to a psych hospital when I missed an appointment with her. I recently found out from my mother, that she would have had me admitted to a hospital if I didn't have a place to go and feel safe like my brother's house. She also prescribed a new medication called Risperdal. I didn't know it was new, or how little they knew about the medication. I was on one-quarter of a normal dose, and it still rocked me. It made me hungry, which made me fat, and it made me super tired.

I was so tired that I would leave school at lunchtime almost every day. I would then eat and go to sleep. I missed so much of my last class that I would have flunked out if my teacher hadn't been kind enough to work with me once she became aware of my circumstances.

Risperdal is an antipsychotic and should be monitored with blood work to ensure adverse side effects are mitigated. I was never told to get regular blood work done, and I got some of the rare

side effects within the first few months. It took years for that to heal and it is still sensitive at times. I went along with what needed to happen while I was home, but as soon as I left for college, I got a second opinion. I was still convinced I had been misdiagnosed and hoped it was situational. I wasn't ready to accept my diagnosis.

2

Early Warning Signs

As a child, I dealt with a great deal of anxiety. I often wouldn't want to go out at all because I didn't want to have to get ready quickly and feel rushed. I also needed a great deal of time alone to recuperate after dealing with a large group of people. Although I learned to love being around people, I still need time to myself to feel sane.

I loved being alone, and I often asked to stay home rather than go along with my mother on outings. By the time I was five, I often got my wish. I know part of the reason I liked being alone was that I could choose the TV shows and movies I wanted to watch.

However, a greater reason was my introversion. I had not been diagnosed at that time, but I would have stayed home rather than be rushed. I also preferred to be alone because being with groups was draining, and I needed a lot of time away to recover.

I don't know of any other warning signs from my childhood, but I did have other early symptoms before my diagnosis at age 17. I started having symptoms when I was 14, in the summer before I started high school.

I was very depressed, and that was when I had my first crash. I had a lot of guilt, and the depression lasted most of that fall, winter, and spring. My parents caught these signs early, and I visited a psychologist weekly during that fall. He was very helpful, and I learned many coping techniques that I still use today (more on those later).

My mom was the first to see my cycles and the bipolar roller coaster for what it is. She would see me depressed one day and super excited the next. During my sophomore year of high school, I had a full up and down cycle about once a month. She could clearly see it and got me in to see a psychiatrist that year. Unfortunately, my psychiatrist still missed the diagnosis.

3

Defining Bipolar

Bipolar is made up of three general phases. One is depression, which is a range from disinterest to serious depression with constant suicidal thoughts. Another is the flip side which ranges from hypomania to severe mania. The final phase is a middle ground or "normal" stage. I will describe each of these phases in more detail, to provide context for those who don't deal with bipolar themselves. I also want to clarify for those who have bipolar, but may not have researched the diagnosis or lived with it long.

The beginning of my depression started with an immediate change from everything feeling okay, to not wanting to get out of bed and feeling awful about myself. This first stage involves a large amount of guilt, shame, shock at being depressed again, and analyzing. Recently the amount of guilt has decreased dramatically, and the shock and shame are basically non-existent[1]. I will share more about how I have accomplished this. I still do a lot of analyzing, mostly because it is the best time to work on adjusting my plans to help manage my

---

[1] See Balancing Your Bipolar : Depression. While this was true at the time, I still have bipolar. When I wrote this book I was in a hypomanic phase. I still believe what I wrote is true, but you have to take it from the perspective it was given, as someone in a hypomanic phase. Everything has rose colored glasses as the lens. I still have guilt during depression etc. Although it is true that it has decreased as I learn to have more balance.

hypomania. Before I accepted my diagnosis, I was met with a hefty dose of disappointment every time I went down. It was like I had failed and it was another nail in the coffin that I actually had bipolar, and I could no longer run from the depression.

In the middle of the depression, it is an endurance marathon that tests everything I have. It is the time to use all the different strategies I have acquired up to that point to help make the depression the best it can be. I work on doing at least one productive thing so I can feel like I did my best and had a worthwhile day. I also try to at least move to the couch from my bed. Because if I don't, I start to feel trapped in my room, like I will never get out of bed and am in an endless loop.

I work to get rid of all unnecessary obligations and expectations and bring them down to a bare minimum. I also tend to stay inside as much as possible because I'm not all that interested in socializing with other people. I'm more self-conscious and anxious and being around other people requires me to try to paint on a face. It is a relief to be able to just live and be happy with the way life is at home.

In the lowest point of the depression, my self-control and willpower have run out. None of the strategies are making a difference anymore, and I'm just tired. This is the time when I want to get medication because it seems so unfair to my family to have to live with me like that. It is also when I want to run away and just disappear, and it seems my family would be better off without me.

I don't mean this in the sense of suicide, which is more common with bipolar individuals than the general population. For me, I have not had any serious suicidal ideations. It is more like I want to be away from reach in a beautiful field with no cell phones or people. I also wonder why I had kids because I have no empathy for them and can no longer think about anyone but myself and all the pain that I'm feeling.

I notice that it is extremely difficult during this time to keep my faith in God. It just feels like nothing works and it isn't worth trying because nothing can get me out of this abyss that feels like it will never end. Luckily, it always does end, and sometimes it feels like the flip side is a blessing.

During the end of the depression, right before it gets easier and better, I start to be in some sort of mixed state. In the mornings I'm depressed, and it is hard to get out of bed, but at night I start to feel some hope and make plans for how to make the next day better. I know that once I start to feel like this I just have to be patient and one day I will actually be able to do the things that I'm planning and wanting to do during those evenings.

I also start to make a shift socially. I want to go out, and I want to plan things although I still have anxiety and don't quite want to follow through and do things with people. It is a very frustrating place to be, when I still can't make plans because my anxiety makes it nearly impossible to follow through with them.

The beginning of hypomania is difficult to define. It is after a period of normal activity. At some point, it shifts to high productivity and wanting to take on the world.

Once I realize that I'm shifting into a hypomanic phase, I make sure that my safeguards are in place. One of the biggest signs is all of a sudden wanting to add obligations to my schedule rather than removing them. I try to maintain a steady activity level, regardless of the phase that I am in so that I don't need to rein in the activity too much. I will get into more detail on activity level later. I have strong impulses to say yes to just about anything that I'm asked, and I think of ways that I can make it happen so that I don't have to say no.

I want to be social and visit people, go shopping, to the park, or anything, whereas in the recent past, I didn't want to leave my house for even the smallest of errands. The way that my brain works starts changing during this phase. I start dreaming big again and wanting different things in my life. I look at houses on the real estate app on my phone. I look at shopping apps and add items to my lists. I start arranging outings to visit friends and family. All of these activities are things that I enjoy but glean no joy from when I'm depressed.

In the middle of my hypomanic phases, I seem to have mini ups and downs that help me stay in that productive place for an extended period. I'm able to accomplish this partly because of my self-care that keeps me from going up too fast and self-destructing.

Hypomania can look good on the outside and can even be fun at times. I have often been told that the highs appear beautiful or that people are jealous of how much I can get done or how motivated I am. However, on the inside, it feels out of control. The spiraling emotions and impulses get so tiring to try to control. At the end of the hypomania, it merely gets beyond my capacity and honestly, pretty crazy.

In the past, I have been running from the depression. Running makes it worse because rather than trying to stop it, I was trying to make it continue because I knew the down would be devastating. I would be running so hard, I would stop eating because I would get going and forget that I hadn't eaten until the afternoon.

I feel desperate to keep everything together. I stay home sometimes for days on end even when I want to go out because I don't want to feel guilty about all the crap I might say from pressured speech, which is a classic symptom of hypomania. In the past, my desperation came from trying not to go down, so I didn't have to admit that I truly have bipolar disorder.

One of the scariest things about being out of control is how damaging it is. There are times when I am so scared of what could have happened if things had gone one step farther. I'm not as worried as I maybe should be about myself, but when my kids almost get hurt because of my inattention, it terrifies me and makes me feel horrible.

I should clarify here that the hurt I'm talking about is not abuse. An example that comes to mind is this: One time, in the height of hypomania, I got my mind set on remodeling our walls. I had to remove boards with nails in them from our entire living room, bedroom, and dining room to accomplish this. At first, I left boards with nails in them all over the house as I worked for days. My husband, told me how dangerous it was and that I needed to do something. I acted like it was no big deal and it barely registered because of the hypomania. Normally, I would never be this negligent. This is the level of hurt and accident that I'm referring to.

Thankfully, I have an awesome husband who works to care for our family with me. He removed the boards and helped me see that it would be much better to take out the nails as I go, which would be safer and easier for everyone.

There are many more aspects of hypomania that are destructive rather than productive, contrary to popular uneducated opinion. One of the most frustrating symptoms is over-sharing through over-talking. I hate feeling like people know things about me that I wish I hadn't shared, and that they may be judging me for it, or think that I'm "crazy". I avoid people completely, because I worry that they will remember awkward things about me.

I feel a strong desire to try everything and accept everything. I have a very hard time saying no. I frequently have to evaluate things that I want to do to see if I really have time for it or if it is even a good idea. One of the hardest things about bipolar in my opinion, especially for the younger crowd, is having strong desires to do things that are really bad for us. I want so badly to do things that will turn out horribly. A few examples of this, are spending extra money and racking up credit card debt, going out every day, taking on too many responsibilities, and ignoring my self-care.

It is also unfortunate that my capacity is less than average. Where someone else could maybe stay out all night repeatedly and be fine or take a nap and keep going, I could be thrown into a depression for months.

From the NIMH — https://www.nimh.nih.gov/health/topics/bipolar-disorder/index.shtml

People having a manic episode may:
- Feel very "up," "high," or elated
- Have a lot of energy

- Have increased activity levels
- Feel "jumpy" or "wired"
- Have trouble sleeping
- Become more active than usual
- Talk really fast about a lot of different things
- Be agitated, irritable, or "touchy"
- Feel like their thoughts are going very fast
- Think they can do a lot of things at once
- Do risky things, like spend a lot of money or have reckless sex

People having a depressive episode may:
- Feel very sad, down, empty, or hopeless
- Have very little energy
- Have decreased activity levels
- Have trouble sleeping, they may sleep too little or too much
- Feel like they can't enjoy anything
- Feel worried and empty
- Have trouble concentrating
- Forget things a lot
- Eat too much or too little
- Feel tired or "slowed down"
- Think about death or suicide

4

Onset

My first crash happened the summer before high school. I basically had a nervous breakdown. I don't remember having a high before going down. However, I definitely remember the guilt. It was cumbersome and it was the first time I went to the people I knew and apologized for things that people wouldn't usually apologize for. That I wouldn't usually apologize for either such as, misspoken words, perceived hurt feelings, etc. Incidents that I was only over analyzing in my own mind.

I would get this guilt and feel like I had to make things right. I scared my childhood best friend. I didn't see her much that summer, and although we were still friends once freshman year started, she had other friends too, when it had mostly just been us before that. I didn't maintain the relationship well.

This was also the start of puberty and changes related to it. I was 14 and little did I know, puberty can be a trigger for bipolar. After that, it took three years before I was officially diagnosed. At this point, I just wanted to be normal, and since I didn't know anything different, I didn't think I was dealing with more than average teenage issues.

I started going through mini ups and downs about every few weeks during freshman year. This was the beginning of my getting way too little sleep. I would be up half the night unable to fall asleep from anxiety, and then I would have dreams (that were all too real) about the next day, and live out my fears in my dreams. I would wake up the following day, sometimes unable to tell whether it had really happened or not. It was silly things like forgetting my homework or math tests that were strange, but vivid. I could only sleep well during the day.

5

Trigger

Right before I was finally diagnosed, I had been up for a while in what I would later learn was hypomania. I was ignoring my responsibilities and the fact that things were getting too hard and overwhelming for me. Inevitably, it all came crashing down. I don't like not having control of my life, but it is a consistent theme.

I was prescribed hydrocodone following my wisdom teeth removal. The first night on hydrocodone, my room looked like it was jumping out to get me. I wasn't quite hallucinating, but things weren't right. I started reliving my fears of salt water and drowning. I had to swish with salt water to keep infection away from my mouth, and it was awful.

I had this fear to begin with, but the salt water and the drugs heightened it to the point where I was having trouble sleeping. Eating was difficult too because everything had to be soft. So here I was not eating well and hardly sleeping at all. The breaking point came when I wanted to run away from home because I just could not sit still. I felt like I was crawling out of my skin.

My dad was out of town at the time on a business trip, and I was struggling with my mom. She told me recently that I thought she was trying to kill me. I still don't remember that. There are times during hypomania that I don't recall; as though my brain doesn't process them into memories. She called a couple of people from church to comfort me. With their help, I was able to calm down enough to stay put and keep going.

During this episode, we went to see my general practitioner before getting in to see the psychiatrist. He was not convinced that anything was wrong but did state that the medication may have taken away my last shred of self-control, which is exactly what it felt like. Control is crucial for me. I absolutely hate feeling out of control.

6

Creating My Own Normal

Classes

I started college a trimester early, at 17, before high school graduation. In hindsight, I probably should have taken lighter loads with my depression and asked for more accommodations. However, at that time I wasn't ready to let people know that I was not "normal".

In my next semester being married at college, I passed half my classes and failed the other half. I did the same thing the next semester and was put on academic probation. Looking back, I was depressed almost the whole fall and winter.

The first fall semester being married, I got a 3.82 and managed well, even being married and working. I continued to get reasonable grades, all above a C, for the rest of my degree and ended up having just a year left, after having my first baby. I took one online class at a time before finally finishing in August 2015. But I did it, and I now have a bachelor's degree in business management with an emphasis in organizational behavior and human resources.

I share this to show that college is doable for bipolar individuals. You may need to make accommodations or adjustments and create your own normal, but it is worth it to reach for whatever it is you want.

Friends

My first semester at school I met Stephanie, she was my first roommate, and I loved hanging out with her. I was still running from my diagnosis, and I had a hard time not moving on out of embarrassment. As for the people I really screwed up with and embarrassed myself with, I just tried to cut contact with them entirely and move on.

I am friends with most of them on social media, but that is the extent of my contact now. It was too hard to stay put and try to work through a whole cycle. If I embarrassed myself when I was up I would just run. I didn't bother trying to fix it because I felt people wouldn't want to be friends with me or that they would judge me for my poor behavior. It was hard to face my mistakes and own up to them. Also, I had bad experiences in the past with over-apologizing, and people finding me crazy. I didn't want to go there again.

Dating

I dated a number of men for short periods of time, no longer than three weeks, before meeting my husband. I wasn't willing to get hurt, and so I avoided investing any more time in relationships. Also, most of the men I dated weren't interested in hanging out for more than a date or two. I was all over the place and not very stable. I even signed up for an online dating site at one point, which was much less acceptable in 2007. You have to be willing to love and respect yourself before you can expect the same from someone else.

After the online dating site, I decided to take a break from guys all together and become happy with myself and being single. It's impressive how often this tactic works, and you get what you want by being happy with your current situation. If you are unhappy with something and decide to become okay with the situation, things start changing. This was the case with me and when I stopped trying so hard for a boyfriend, I had multiple guys ask me out (including my soon-to-be husband).

Marriage

Our marriage is built on honesty. When we first started dating, I was having trouble talking with my husband about an important issue. He kept asking me until I told him what was bothering me. Before this, I had only had relationships that lasted a few weeks because I chose to run instead of communicating. Conrad knew, and told me later, that if we couldn't communicate about this issue, we wouldn't make it. Since then, we have been very honest in our relationship. We push each other to share even when it is hard. He is very patient with me when my first instinct is to run and hide from a situation.

For almost a year, Conrad worked at a crisis care behavioral hospital. He learned a lot of empathy there and more information on how to care for people struggling with their mental health. I am so grateful for this time and how it helped him to understand that you can't just snap out of it. It is also really nice to know that if anything were to ever go super crazy, we have a plan that we can take my kids to be with my mom and he can take care of me before I would have to go to a hospital.

Because we are taking a holistic approach to handling bipolar, without medication, we have to be prepared for extreme situations. It gives me peace of mind to know that we will be able to act quickly to keep our family safe if we need to.

I struggle with feeling out of control and he helps me push the boundaries. One of the ways we stretched my limit was for him to tickle me to the point where I could no longer stand it, and then he would hold me while I cried from the excess of emotion. Although it was difficult for me, it was good for our trust in one another and to expand my comfort zone. Recently I remembered a time when I was 5 or 6 when I was thrown into a pool by an adult who thought I could swim. I couldn't even float, and sat under the water blowing bubbles.

That is all I had learned to do. I was pulled up but I think that may be a small part of why I fear things like sudden unexpected touch.

Conrad is the one person who truly sees my ups and downs and can help me to filter and distinguish reality. Without him, I wouldn't have learned nearly as much about myself and my phases. We frequently have conversations about how things went during my up, right after I go down. That is the time when I'm most receptive and still remember my ups clearly. It is painful to talk about, but after not listening to Conrad for a while, we need to reconnect.

During depression, I check with him about text messages and my feelings to see if I'm filtering correctly. It is shocking to me how often I'm not! However, I'm getting better at learning to see when I'm not filtering my thoughts correctly and adjust based on the truth from past experience. This is making it so I handle some scenarios myself by combining past experience and applying it to the current situation.

He supports me relentlessly in a good way. He does this by helping me stick to my true goals, which is something I really struggle with when I'm hypomanic. I tend to be impulsive like a teenager and focus more on short-term goals and instant gratification than my long-term true goals.

He keeps me grounded, which is something I can't do for myself well. He encourages me gently to manage my activity levels by making suggestions. He doesn't completely take away any of my choices though, and simply provides a voice of reason and an extra check to help me stick to my goals. Sometimes this feels like tough love, and I don't like it in the moment. This is mainly because of the hypomania. But I'm so grateful especially on the flip side.

Hormones

Hormones throw a wrench in bipolar and make everything spiral out of control. It is hard to predict, really impossible, how I will react during each pregnancy and postpartum period.

The hormones of my pregnancies are affecting my emotional state more and more. Each pregnancy has been worse than the one before. I don't know if it is just because I have other children to care for and so pregnancy is just more demanding of me, but they are definitely getting worse. I still want to have more children, but I'm starting to wonder if adoption might be a better option if we decide to add to our family.

My first pregnancy was really relaxed. I maybe had one week of depression in the whole thing and it was situational. We had just moved while working and going through finals, and it was an overdose of stress.

I was worried about postpartum, because of my bipolar, and watched it closely afterward. I noticed a little bit of depression but I think it was my regular ups and downs slightly accentuated by interrupted sleep. I mentioned it to my doctor as it was about a year after I had my baby. Unfortunately he was a GP, and didn't pay much attention to my chart or just didn't know, but he prescribed an SSRI (selective serotonin reuptake inhibitor), commonly used as an antidepressant, that shouldn't be prescribed to bipolar people without a mood stabilizer.[2] It took my depression, that I was starting to come out of, and dragged me into one of the worst downs that I have ever had. I stopped taking it within a month and that was the last time I have medicated my mental illness. I have only been on two medications for bipolar ever and neither improved my health or coping long-term.[3]

As for my second pregnancy, I had a really good second trimester, where I killed it in my business and was super up (hypomanic) at the time. After that, I sunk into a three month long depression for the whole end of the pregnancy. It was so bad that I just laid in bed.

I snapped out of that depression after delivery and didn't really have

---

[2] I recently found out that this is actually one that usually works well for bipolar disorder. The general practitioner wasn't incompetent at all.

[3] This is no longer true. I have tried a new one and it is working well. See Balancing Your Bipolar: Depression.

postpartum. The only weirdness that I experienced was being so tired that I kept giving the baby back to Conrad after I fed her. One day when I woke up, I felt like I didn't love my baby, and I was so sad. But then I held her and I started playing with her and I fell in love instantly. I just needed to get to know her a little better.

My most recent pregnancy was much harder, hormonally, than I remember any of the others being. The second trimester was definitely the hardest. I was all over the place emotionally. I was up and down and in some kind of mixed state. I remember screaming at my two year old for no good reason. It was so ridiculous but I couldn't break out of it. Luckily, Conrad was there and pulled me away and told me to go take care of what was stressing me out. Managing stress is a huge part of bipolar, and why so many of the tools I share later are essential.

Parenting

One of the greatest things about being a parent is how much it changes you for the better. Kids are the greatest teachers and help parents learn the lessons they need to learn. My kids are often the reason I get out of bed. I can't just stay in bed or they are all over me, asking for food and to play, etc. This is a good thing some times and a difficult thing during others. My children are definitely a reason for me to keep going, but kids also bring a base level of stress that makes life more complex. I try my best to care for them even when I am feeling poorly. Even if it is just moving to the couch from my bed, I make an effort to be there for them.

My temper with my hypomania is a force to be reckoned with. I have tried, on numerous occasions, to take yelling out of our home. I believe I have made progress but it does still happen. We are working on a new parenting strategy, *Love & Logic,* that is giving great results and I'm hoping it will help with some of the indecision that leads to yelling. It is hard with my irritability from hypomania to completely stop the yelling. It escapes my control sometimes and makes me very sad.

One of the hardest things that I struggle with is consistency. When I go through the various cycles, sometimes I'm too depressed to parent because it just isn't worth the effort. Although, I'm realizing it's harder not to deal with it than experience the pain and fear of facing my emotions. However, the even bigger problem is, when I'm super hypomanic, and I don't want to deal with any problems at all. I do whatever I can to avoid a blow-up or anything I have to deal with, so I try to stop the problems before they happen with a lot of permissive parenting. This is something I am, of course, working on in many ways. We are significantly decreasing the number of television shows we allow in our home on a daily basis, and I'm working on strategies to make parenting easier and to increase my level of consistency.

Jobs

All of the jobs I have had since having kids have been work-from-home so I could stay home with my family. I refuse to work outside the home and we really work to make this possible. I can't hold down a traditional job well, especially with my choice to forego medication and use natural methods of balance. Part of these natural methods consist of working to create a life that is calm and conducive to them.

I am attracted, as many bipolar people are, to multilevel marketing opportunities and the allure of unlimited income related to network marketing. When I am hypomanic, I want to talk to everyone and have visions of grandeur. It is easy to think that I will be successful with each new venture. It hasn't turned out that way, and since I tend to sign up for extra work when I'm hypomanic, I would always crash and dislike the jobs when I became depressed.

I found MTurk, an Amazon-based crowd-sourcing platform, and it has been a totally different experience than my previous work from home jobs that worked best when I was hypomanic and not at all when depressed. It was less than successful at first, only making pennies because I didn't understand how it all worked. Luckily, I kept at it and found more information on Reddit, guides and other information that really helped me turn it around and start earning fair pay and making a difference in our income.[4]

What surprised me the most about this job was how well it worked as a therapeutic technique. Also, you can work as much as you want as long as there is work and you literally have no minimum requirements. So when I didn't want to work, I didn't have to, and when I wanted to, even at 3 am, I was able to.

It is a great way to calm the crazy and channel my fidgeting and irritability into something much more productive than puzzle apps, games, and reading. I feel good about myself after working and earning money for our family. When I am depressed, it stops the negative chatter in my mind. I have to pick easier jobs that require less focus and thinking, but I can do the mindless sorting tasks while watching Netflix and still make a big difference. It also gives me a feeling of accomplishment that helps me break out of the depression more quickly. This is a job that I still use and will probably continue to use for a while as a side job. For more information visit my blog post on the subject.

I started blogging in June 2017 as a potential way to make income and get my thoughts out there. I was originally going to write memoir posts and then compile them into a book, and I did a little of that before deciding to write the book first to help get the word out. I was amazed at the reception, and at my friends who popped out of the woodwork, confiding that they also suffered from bipolar. I love chatting with and helping some of them. It is definitely something I can do whether I'm up or down or in-between, since it provides different perspectives.

---

[4] I have written a blog post including the guide that I created from my research into running Mturk for yourself.

https://balancingmybipolar.wordpress.com/2018/06/05/amazon-mechanical-turk-review-plus-guide-to-get-started/

II

Road to Acceptance

7

Acceptance

During the months leading up to finally accepting my diagnosis, I was growing more and more hypomanic. The longer I delay self-care, the worse it gets, and unfortunately, the worse the depression is afterward. The depression tends to mirror the hypomania and be proportionally about as bad as the high. The peak of the worst of my hypomania, before I accepted my diagnosis, was during my family reunion and it was ridiculous. I cringe when I think of that experience and how out of control my emotions were.

Previous to the reunion, I learned of energy work from my mother-in-law and became a certified practitioner. I had been introduced by other friends a few years earlier but didn't have too much interest in it. It helped a little bit but I hadn't seen any lasting effects until I started working with my mother-in-law. I had some great experiences and really liked how I felt when the negative emotions were released. I was much more open and I felt amazing for quite awhile. I was up from February 2015 until the end of August 2015. I got my energy work certification in July, right after completing my bachelor's degree, which was my self-imposed requirement.

Part of the reason I wanted to get it done so quickly was to help out my mother-in-law. She was being inundated with work and could use help with a partner who was able to take over some of the clients. I ended up trying to start my own practice, but only helped one paid client before I got too depressed to be able to continue, and finally stopped promoting my business.

The people that I helped were very appreciative. The large majority felt that it made a huge difference and I had people messaging me for months, thanking me for the difference it made in their anxiety or pain management. This wasn't just family members that I helped, but friends of friends that I was able to assist.

The family reunion was in the middle of all of this, at the beginning of August. We traveled to the Oregon coast, close to where I grew up. The reunion was mostly for me, Conrad supported me super well. He was kind and hung out with us but mainly watched kids so I could enjoy it. However, I remember very little of it, because I was hypomanic, and mostly just remember the offenses I felt from being emotionally sensitive and all over the place. Luckily, my girls had a really good time, and my oldest still remembers it as a positive experience that she wants to repeat.

Once I came home from the family reunion, I went out for one more weekend to a party in Salt Lake City with my family before I was down for the count. I started falling quickly and went deeper and deeper into depression for weeks, before I stopped functioning all together for months. During this time, the energy work wasn't enough to keep me from crashing. That had always been the goal in the past with trying new techniques and this time wasn't any different. I bought in 100% to the idea that this could cure my bipolar if I believed in it enough, was positive enough, and continued to release negative emotions.

I got extremely desperate at the end, but it didn't matter what I did. I wasn't able to keep the crash from coming. After I crashed, I came home to Conrad and finally started listening again. I distanced myself from the energy work until I could distinguish between the hypomania and the truth. I finally decided that the energy work is useful for focusing my energy and putting a name to the emotions that I'm experiencing so I can let go of them. In 2017, nearly two years later I started using energy work again. This is especially helpful when

I'm angry and can't put my finger on the reason. It helps me to let go of the negative emotions by trying to put a name to them. It has been very effective, and I feel it is a great therapy technique.

I was finally able to accept my diagnosis in this crash. I accepted that I couldn't run from it any longer. I have bipolar and I can make a difference. Instead of trapping me further, it was actually very empowering to stop playing the victim card and open up to the idea that my choices can help make my illness better. Instead of saying, "Well, I couldn't help myself because I *am* bipolar," I could say, "Yes, I *have* bipolar and hypomania, but I can set up safeguards to help me make the choices that I want to make."

It is a night and day difference between my previous episodes and what I experience now. The downs only last for a couple of days, except when I'm pregnant, which throws hormones into the mix and make things extremely unpredictable. When not pregnant, however, I haven't had a major down since accepting my diagnosis, which has now been over two years. I have a lot of mini ups and downs, but I am very serious about not overexerting myself, plus protecting my self-care practices, and it is working!

III

Finding Balance

8

Sleep

Depression

During depression, sleep is often out of balance. Up late from anxiety, sleep in, take naps. Normally, it is during the day rather than the night, which can still be very problematic. It often throws off my well-crafted sleep schedule. I was told as a teen not to take naps so that I would be able to sleep at night, but that didn't work for me. I would just continue to sleep less and less because my anxiety for the next day overruled my need for sleep.

Now, I nap when I need to, and work in sleep any way that I can. I also work hard to increase my level of self-care and let myself rest. Depression, in many ways, reflects hypomania because it is repairing the damage that was caused during hypomania. I let myself sleep extra and significantly decrease my obligations to allow myself to heal from any damage from the months before.

When I'm depressed, my anxiety at night often prevents me from falling asleep on time. As soon as it gets late, I get terrified of the day ahead and worry about what comes next, rather than letting go of what I can't control and letting it wait for the next day. I used to let this go on until three or four in the morning. Now, I work to get myself to sleep earlier, through effective routines, and canceling obligations.

Hypomania

When hypomanic, sleep is a whole different story. Rather than managing oversleeping, I have to make sure I get *enough* rest and work harder to wind down because my body wants to keep moving all the time. One of the things I do to protect my sleep and force myself to rest is to take days off where all I do is lie in bed, watch shows, eat, and fall asleep whenever I feel the need. This works well to keep me grounded and stop me from getting too little sleep. If I get too high, I stop sleeping as well. I sometimes stop napping and sleep goes to only 5-6 hours per night. I know many people have it worse.

It is harder to sleep in when I'm hypomanic. Although I can often work to fall asleep at a reasonable time and get on a schedule, it is very hard to control staying asleep. I often find myself waking up at three in the morning for a few hours or waking up at 5:30 a.m. and continuing to get less and less sleep, which creates a deficit that eventually needs to be reconciled. This can happen from a depression, which makes me extra tired, or from a self-imposed day of rest that allows me to sleep when I need to, by forcing myself from all activities so that I can feel how tired I truly am.

Self-Care

Sleep is a huge part of wellness for everyone, but even more so for people with mental illness. If my sleep gets too far off it makes functioning extremely difficult. I feel like my 'stereotypical crazy' comes out in full force, especially when I'm hypomanic and sleep less. I become more of the irrational, dangerous teenager seeing myself as invincible. This is tame, I know, compared to some. For me, it is irrational and dangerous compared to when I'm a responsible adult. For example, once I went to a friends house while nine months pregnant at 9 p.m. and was out until 11:30 p.m. without telling my husband that I would be staying longer, and I wasn't answering my phone.

Self-care is essential because it is all about loving myself enough to care about taking steps before problems arise. This is very difficult to do especially when it feels like I'm not only fine, but better than ever. I have to listen to my loved ones who can see that what I'm doing is not normal for me, and in fact, is hurting my body and my long-term goals.

Tools to Help

This is where the tools to help me sleep come in, and we will talk about implementing them. One of the strategies that I like best when I'm up, is a *brain dump*. This can be as simple as writing down a to-do list for the next day. It can be done physically or digitally and works well either way. When you're dealing with anxiety and/or low levels of sleep, memory becomes a big issue and writing things down is very important. This also decreases anxiety because you know that you won't forget, and you can stop running a constant loop of all the things that you need to remember.

A routine (just like you would have for a young child) can be very helpful as well. Our brains love repetition. The more you have a habit and a schedule, the longer it lasts during the times that it is difficult to stick to a routine. I find when I have little sleep, my reticular activation system, which keeps these routines running without having to think about it, breaks down.

It is still worthwhile to have a routine because it does make some difference in all the phases. I like to have a wind-down routine. Once I get in bed, I turn off the lights, curl up, and read my scriptures. Then I *mind dump*, say a prayer as I fall asleep with gratitude, and if I'm not sleeping yet, when I'm feeling well I try to dream. I imagine my dreams and desires as though they were real. It is a good way to relax and keep my brain focused on one idea, so my thinking helps me sleep rather than keeping me awake.

When there is no anxiety, I'm able to read to sleep. I can't stay awake, to be honest. I simply read for a very short period, even half a page, and I'm so tired that I drop my phone. One thing that really helps with this is using the night setting with white writing in my kindle and the lights off. I also have an app on my phone called *twilight* that filters out blue light which keeps you awake. It's

so dark that I sometimes can't see the text, but when it is at just the right setting, it encourages relaxation.

When my anxiety just won't let me sleep, one of my go-to strategies is to ask my spouse for a massage. My favorite is when he plays with my hair and rubs my back and shoulders. Not everyone has this luxury, but your kids can play with your hair to help you relax. Another option is to take a bath or use a foot massager. I have found that having my hair played with is my personal favorite. Turning off the TV and electronics a few hours before bed may help to wind your mind down as well.

Another strategy that I love is from a blog post called *Drops of Awesome:* http://dropsofawesome.com/drops-of-awesome/. I found the post a few years ago, and it was valuable to me during my depressions. The idea is to love yourself and let the little things count. I would write down the things that were amazing that day, before going to bed, and be grateful for them. It also helps during the day to tell myself drops of awesome when I do something no matter how small. It helps me keep going and combat negative thoughts. This helped me fall asleep on many occasions. More on this later in chapter 14, section Love Yourself.

Suggested Sleep Routine

- Turn off the lights
- Feed yourself spiritually (flip this for first if you don't use a device or have a bedside lamp)
- *Mind dump*

- Focus on gratitude and count your blessings
- Dream and imagine your ideal life

9

Food

Nutrition

Nutrition is important to me. I have wanted to be powerful and keep my body in a condition where I can play any sport that I want. To do that, I need to be eating healthily, and I want to live a long healthy life. However, I also realize that to survive, eating something is better than eating nothing, and will keep me alive long enough to eat healthily when I can.

Sometimes I am only interested in sweets. I eat a brownie and cream cheese frosting every day for weeks or even months. I know that it is not good nutritionally, but it seems that it is all I *can* eat. I have to tell myself that something is better than nothing and enjoy eating it. When nothing sounds good or tastes good, it is a relief to be able to eat without force-feeding myself or gagging on every other bite.

Ways that I try to eat healthier, however, are also important. One of the ways I eat healthier is to prepare meals that I know I will like when I'm depressed. I do this when I'm hypomanic, and love cooking and often overcook, and the food would go to waste.

Instead of wasting that food and my time, I cook freezer meals. Then it makes my life easier during the times that I don't want to cook. I also figure my burritos, taquitos etc. are probably much healthier (and cheaper) than the store version.

Another strategy I use, is to try to eat dinner as a family and, at least, get in one good, nutritious meal that doesn't just consist of treats. When all else fails, and I can barely do anything, often during depression, I meal plan with Conrad, consulting the freezer to decide a menu for the next seven days. That way we can pull things out of the freezer, so they are ready, and not have to think about food longer than necessary.

Processed foods are often part of the easy, low prep comfort foods that I crave no matter what phase I'm in. The only time that I don't is when I really want to cook new things each day. Making my own versions of the processed foods has helped with cost and nutrition. I try to focus on things that I can eat repeatedly so that I can make them in bulk and know I will use them.

One day I would love to try out a ketogenic diet. A ketogenic diet is a low-carb, high-fat diet taken to the extreme of 20 net carbs or less a day, mainly from vegetables. There are many resources online. Some of these resources suggest that reducing or eliminating sugar (which is what this diet does) can help bipolar.

Texture

For some reason, when I'm depressed, texture is uncomfortable for me in any variety. I need things to be simple and easy to process, or I can't get them past my throat. The food needs to be easy to chew and easy to go down, or it often won't happen.

I recently read about a condition called Avoidant/Restrictive Food Intake Disorder (AFRID). I think just from a first look, this could be what I have. However, I don't lose a great deal of weight. Also, I only really have it when I'm depressed. It is the closest thing I have come across that sounds like what I go through.

Most things need to be basic. I rely on foods like pizza, bagels and cream cheese, pudding, toast, and basic smoothies. These foods are familiar and easy to eat. I always try to add protein and high-fat content to my smoothies to make them last longer and be more worthwhile as they are very easy to ingest.

It never ceases to amaze me how strong this texture issue has control over my body. One day I was hypomanic and pushing too hard, but I made a white spinach chicken lasagna, and it was amazing to me in its cheesy goodness. I loved it and ate a big serving. The next day, however, I heated it again for lunch and gagged on every bite before I had to just throw it away. I had crashed in between those two instances, and the texture was no longer appetizing.

One of the symptoms of depression is dry mouth, and it increases as my depression worsens. I'm not sure if it is partly from not drinking enough water, from over-swallowing, or merely a symptom of depression. I do try to use extra liquids, especially with meals. It can be helpful to take a drink whenever it is hard to swallow. At times, I have had to resort to smooth or liquid foods. Smoothies, nut butter, and fruit are foods I have used to get in high calories with minimal chewing.

Eating Issues

I considered titling this section *Eating Disorders*, but I don't like the connotation associated with that term, and I'm not sure that the popular definition of it quite fits the problems I deal with. A few of my friends have shared that they struggle the same way that I do and it doesn't totally embody what I know of eating disorders, such as anorexia or bulimia. It is not that I'm trying to starve myself because I want to, or because I want to be skinnier, look better, or be in control.

Many times, the reason I may eat less food has more to do with not being able to find something to fit into the criteria I listed above, and so instead of eating something disgusting or gagging through it, I choose not to eat instead.

At times, I have been worried about nutrition to the point where I can't decide on a food option because anything worth making seems horribly overwhelming and so I'm stuck in a loop of indecision. Not that I'm trying not to eat, but I can't settle on *what* I want to eat. If anything, I don't think that I'm too fat, I think that I'm too thin, but in some twisted way, that feeds my self-hatred and causes me to be less likely to find the motivation to care for myself and eat sufficiently.

One of the biggest struggles that I have is cooking for my children and me. It feels like such a burden, I have an idea that has been working fairly well recently, which is to cook for them and then cook for myself separately. Sometimes I end up eating with them anyway, which is great because I will probably get more nutrition. Even if I don't and I end up eating cookies or cake for dinner, at least I don't have to feel guilty for ruining my children's nutrition.

Luckily, when I'm pregnant or nursing, I have a much higher appetite, and I'm able to eat much more easily. I have both the motivation to eat more and the appetite too, which encourages me to get the nutrition that I need, but also for the baby who relies on me.

I don't personally deal with overeating. I know many people do, especially with side effects from medication for bipolar. That is valid and very real for some. In those instances, it is important to focus on nutrition, and then work to stick to your long-term goals whenever possible. One way to allow for overeating, while still maintaining, is to utilize a ketogenic diet. As long as you stay low carb, you can eat as much fat as you want. Many people find this helps them lose weight because fat is satiating, and they end up eating less. Be kind to yourself though, and remember, your mental health comes first.

Strategies to Make Eating Easier

- Find go-to foods that always sound good
- Eat what you can, anything is better than nothing
- Make food ahead of time, so you don't have to overthink
- When possible, eat whole, low processed foods

10

Exercise

Endorphins

One of the biggest benefits of exercise for depression and health, in general, is the endorphins that are released. Regular exercise through walking daily or strength training a few times a week requires minimal effort while producing a substantial benefit. Part of fighting depression is getting out of your head. This can also be an incredible tool to help with the irritability that can come from hypomania as well. Sometimes you just need to burn off the excess emotions that come with life. The endorphins make it easier to stay positive and remain in a place of balance.

Strength

One of my goals is to be strong in a functional way. I know that is currently somewhat of a buzzword, but to me, it means that I can care for my children and play with them and play any sport I want when I want to. I also prefer the look of a bodyweight fitness athlete to that of a body builder who can lift heavier weights, but doesn't have the same level of control over his body. Physical play can be a big part of building bonds with children but even in other relationships, playing is a big part of being healthy.

The older you get, the easier it becomes to get injured from pulling muscles or tearing tendons, to breaking your hip when you're in the golden years. Flexibility and strength training as a regular, but reasonable part of your routine, go a long way toward preventing these types of injuries. Often they are due to overestimating your abilities, which doesn't happen as often when you are in control of your body and in tune with it.

Rebuild

When I am depressed, and it gets bad, I can lay on the couch for weeks, if not months, and when I don't eat enough, muscle mass is often the first thing to go. This is also a problem with pregnancies. It gets harder for me to work out when I'm sick, and I'm worried about my tendons being loose and causing injuries.

One of my goals, when I'm hypomanic, is to counter that muscle loss. Part of my routine to manage the energy and restlessness from hypomania, is regular exercise with a goal in mind to make specific progress. Measurable progress helps me to move forward and stick to my goals without getting distracted and trying a number of different programs. This can be measured by the number of reps that I can do in a specific exercise or by increasing the difficulty or time. I have seen huge success with using exercise to rebuild my muscle mass and strength most recently from pregnancy and the havoc that it wreaks with my core muscles.

Ideas/Tips

There is a myriad of strategies to fitness and exercise, and you will need to find what works best for you. Many people have limited time to exercise, in which case, simple moves that have large benefits (like heavy weight lifting) could be best for them. There are also people who have to be careful with injuries or are just starting and may benefit more from repeated exercises with little or no weight. I prefer bodyweight fitness, which can vary from no weight added, like with my current squats, to handstands where my whole body is on my shoulders and wrists.

I use the *beginning fitloop.co routine,* which you can tailor to just about any fitness level. It also requires only three hours a week on alternating days, which works for me. Initially, right after having my last baby, I only did the stretches and core routine which kept the workout to only 30 minutes per week. I did some walking, but this was all the strength I had because I mainly needed to heal my core and back so that I would be able to move on to heavier exercises. Your core is the most essential part of your body, and a strong core will help lessen injuries that you may incur.

Other exercises that people may want to try would be running with your kids while they play at the park or with a jogging stroller or just while playing with them. Another trend would be thirty-day challenges, in the form of the squat and plank challenge.

Another option is to join a sports league which will keep you and your teammates invested and keep you accountable, at least, for the games. You can do this officially or with pick-up games that you can organize. I participated in a group like this that does ultimate frisbee, and I went once a week. Swimming and biking and running are great options as well, but I recommend only trying things like this if you love it or have a goal in mind that you want to reach.

In all these exercises it is important to ease into the workouts and stop when you encounter any pain. Being sore isn't always an indication that you are getting the best results. Also, you want to make sure that you keep your workouts 48-hours apart for the same muscle groups. If you want to work out every day, just keep weight lifting for your upper body on a different day than your lower body. This will ensure that you get the most benefit from your workout.

Exercise Action Steps

- Find a simple routine you can stick to
- Stop when there is any pain
- Always push for more improvement, endurance, intensity, etc.
- Manage expectations, scale back to just walking if needed

11

Activity Level

Limit Daily Activity

After I accepted my diagnosis, I discovered how important it is to limit daily activity to keep from burning out. Especially when I'm hypomanic. The acceptable and achievable daily activity level changes from day to day. The key to making this work is to accept that and adjust your expectations accordingly. If you start the day expecting to knock out ten big things on your to-do list and you can barely make it to the couch, it is hard not to be disappointed and hard on yourself. Instead, if you know the day will be hard you can give yourself one simple but impactful action to accomplish for the day, that will be acceptable to you. Then you can be happy with yourself. At the very least you can accept that it is your best and you tried your hardest. You may be able to do an extra task or two, and that is great. Instead of feeling let down you can be happy and congratulate yourself on going the extra mile.

Another key to making daily activity limits work is to prioritize your activities. This will vary from person to person and may vary by the day or time of life as well. Some suggestions for top priorities would be family, children, spouse, career, and long-term goals.

One of the hardest things for me to keep in check is maintaining progress toward my long-term goals when I am hypomanic. I tend to turn into an impulsive teenager who only thinks of the immediate issues and self-gratification. This isn't conducive to an adult's goals and responsibilities. By prioritizing your activity levels and self-monitoring throughout various phases of life, you can stay on track toward your long-term goals to achieve results. This can be most difficult when you're depressed and have little or no motivation. This is an important time to prioritize as you may only make one or two actions happen in a day. You need those to make an impact and continue moving your goals forward.

It is easy to get tired quickly. I often feel that I tire faster than other people whether I'm up or down. I have to be careful of myself and make sure I keep up with self-care or I can spiral, and be able to do far less. One of the keys to managing a reasonable activity level is not to compare yourself with anyone else. This is difficult for me as I believe it is for most people. However, if you try to compete with people on social media or your peers and friends you will be disappointed and who knows, you may be comparing your worst with their best. I also tend to compare my up self vs. my down self.

One Outing

One of the ways that we have implemented activity-limiting success-fully, has been a self-imposed one outing per week limit. This includes extra activities beyond essential commitments. You can adjust this to meet your needs and capacity. Make sure that you have someone to help remind you if you start veering off and getting too many commitments, but make sure that this is also self-imposed. Many of these strategies won't work if someone else is trying to control your mental illness with them. However, when you decide to accept your diagnosis and work with it, you can empower yourself with responsibility, rather than playing the victim card. I don't say this to hurt anyone's feelings who isn't there yet. It took me 11 years after onset, and seven years from diagnosis, to accept that I have bipolar, so no rush. I found I was much happier after I came to terms with it and much more successful in finding balance.

This one outing excludes essential shopping trips, although I try to keep these to one a week or less to manage our spending (more on this later). It also doesn't include essential church and school obligations. It *does* include extras such as service opportunities and volunteering. This can become excessive, and once again, you have to monitor and prioritize. One exception that we made to accommodate when I'm feeling the need for social interaction, is that I can have anyone over whenever I want. If people come to me, then it isn't included in the one outing a week. I do try to have a day off though if I have had a number of packed days in a row.

Fill Your Vessel

Taking a day at home here and there is one of the best ways that I have found to fill my vessel and keep me from going too high into hypomania and causing myself to crash and burn even deeper into depression. This has been a huge key to my finding balance and creating my own version of normal. This is a self imposed rest day where I stay home and turn on the TV and lie in bed for as long as needed. I watch shows, take naps, eat food when I'm hungry and care for the basics just like I do when I'm depressed. I truly believe depression is mandatory self-care that you can't escape. However, it has its benefits, and filling your vessel is one of them. Books and games are also other options. Meditation and time in nature help as well.

The key is to let yourself relax when all you want to do is go. Break the spiral that can be so destructive, because it can turn from productive to harmful without your noticing.

Everything will survive without you. You are important and valued, but remember, there is always someone else, and it's okay to let them step in for you for a short period while you look out for number one.

How to Say NO

It is okay to use your illness when you need to opt out of something or a request from someone. It is an illness after all, no matter what phase you are in. If you had a broken hip, no one would expect you to play sports, and it is okay to treat your illness accordingly. It is also okay to push your boundaries sometimes and grow and stretch. But be careful that no one is trying to manipulate you into doing so for their own gain. Also, make sure you are practicing good self-care and saying no is a big part of that.

Just know that others will fill the gap. Almost all organizations are set up with a number two, and you probably shouldn't be in that number one spot if you are still trying to find balance in your life and don't know where your limits are. My church leaders and I have agreed that if I hit a depression, and am having a hard time making it to church and my obligations are making it harder to attend, that I can say the word and remove that obligation, no questions asked. I have had to use this on occasion, and it was very helpful. It allowed me to continue to attend church with less anxiety. There are other people who are in a better place to serve, and you will be there one day to fill the gap for others as well. It is okay to lean on other people.

Right now, I'm telling you to let go of the guilt you feel building up just because you are *thinking* about saying no. If you don't have this guilt, cheers for you, you're on your way. If you do, know that it is okay and it can get better. This guilt isn't helpful for you or anyone else. No one who loves you wants you to feel this way, and it only holds you back, it doesn't help you get stronger. If you have to practice, do so, like in *27 Dresses,* find someone to ask you questions and practice saying *no.* Make some of them ridiculous to get you started and then work on harder ones, but get used to saying no and taking care of yourself.

Find what works best for you. It could be, "that doesn't work for me." It could be blunter, as I have had to be at times, "I have bipolar, so I don't do that." If you aren't ready to reveal that, it is ok to say "I'm sick" or "I'm busy". This is a personal preference and should eventually become easy to say and leave you guilt-free knowing you are taking care of yourself for yourself and your family.

Steps to a Rest Day

- Remove all obligations from your day
- Choose a relaxing activity (i.e., read a book, watch shows, take a nap, walk in nature, meditation)
- Keep food readily available
- Lay down so you can easily sleep
- Get a babysitter if you need to

12

Medications

Balance

For many bipolar individuals, balance is elusive on so many levels. I know this is also an issue for people without this diagnosis. Sometimes especially in hypomania, it is easy to let go of all the good habits you have worked so hard to create because everything moves so quickly. I can go hours without remembering to eat and feeling like I have to do just one more thing. It is also difficult to stay asleep when my mind is going a million miles an hour. This is where medication can be helpful to aid in balance when it gets too hard to get back on track. Many people think that the depression is the most damaging side of bipolar and that may be true for some, and suicide is an especially scary symptom of depression. However, hypomania can be terribly dangerous because it is so irrational and unpredictable mania is even more so.

After my diagnosis, my medication, Risperdal, was a life saver. Although I don't love medication, and I don't feel that it is worth it for me at this point. It was very helpful to get me eating and sleeping again when I didn't know how to navigate the basics with the level of chaos I was experiencing. I don't want to go through the trouble of finding a medication that works and all the pain that can be. I frequently think about medication and I'm open to the option if it ever gets to a point where I'm too dangerous to myself or others, or the pain I'm going through is worse than the side effects would be. If I were always up or down, it would be easier for me to bite that bullet. I have talked with people who are in that position, and I know it is still a difficult decision.

Selection

I have to be honest; I have very little experience with this. I have been on medications twice since my diagnosis. Once at the beginning, for about five months, and I went off cold turkey, because I was on such a low dose of Risperdal, like half a pill. The other time was just after my first baby and I was struggling a little with postpartum depression, the first big depression since being married. I went to my general practitioner and didn't give him enough background because I was desperate. He prescribed some SSRI (I don't even remember what it was called). All that I remember is that it threw me into a horrible depression when I was coming out of it. I was only on it for about a month before I went off.

Since then, I have stuck to trying to find other ways to manage my highs and lows, and as I learn new techniques for balance, I add them to my tool belt. When you fight for long periods to keep balance in your life, you need all the help you can get.

Long-Term

I am definitely open to medication for the long-term. I don't want to totally rule out options when I make my decisions. My husband and family support me in finding my own version of normal, and making it work the best for me. If life ever gets too horrible or isn't working for me the way that I want, I'm free to try the medication route. I have heard many people say bipolar gets worse as you get older and that is definitely a fear for me. In my opinion, that is because medications have awful side effects and don't always work the same the longer you are on them (and if you get used to them). However, please never take anything I say about medication to be any kind of professional opinion. I'm one person, with an admittedly mild case of bipolar, forging my own path with the help of an amazing support system. I always recommend anyone with questions about medication seek help from medical professionals.

Consult a Professional

This leads me to my next section on consulting medical professionals. Whether you work with a psychiatrist, general practitioner, or another medical professional, that is a personal decision and a relationship that I can't be a part of. I'm not a medical professional and have no professional training. This is my disclaimer, and I'm going the extra mile because I don't want anyone hurting themselves by trying to follow my footsteps in too much of an extreme.

These steps and systems for balance have been ten years in the making, added one at a time. I have experimented with what works for me, and I desire to provide hope and direction in a time of turmoil such as a new diagnosis. I *don't* suggest that anyone quit their medications. I *do* suggest you stay in close contact with medical professionals, and advocate for your own health, or get someone you trust to do it for you.

Tips with Medication

- Consult your Physician
- Don't be afraid to ask for adjustments
- Stick to your schedule
- See my second book Balancing Your Bipolar: Depression, for

further information as my views on medication have shifted with increased personal experience.

13

Personal Finance

Balance

One thing I want to get out of the way from the beginning is that it is okay to have wants and desires beyond our basic needs. However, when someone is hypomanic, they want things based on impulsive desires. Often, I don't even want the things I buy just a day or two later. Unless I had it on a list from the past, I normally don't want it once I shift into a different phase or come down to a middle ground.

I hope to provide some tools to help you regain control of your true wants and desires and help you stick to those goals. We all have wants and needs, but we need to preserve resources for those actual wants and needs, not the excess that we feel helps us seem successful or happy. I honestly think it really boils down to increased speed in decision making increased impulse and decreased control.

One thing that I have found in trying to rein in spending is that it is smarter to monitor and budget and put up blocks to help think things through, than it is to cut spending completely. When I tell myself I can't spend anything for super long periods of time, I tend to splurge and it is often worse than it would have been to set a reasonable budget. I do, however, find that short periods of spending breaks, like 30 days, can be very valuable to regain perspective.

A reasonable amount of play money keeps me from using essential income for things that don't meet my long-term goals and aren't my true desires. This is intended to be a moderate amount, but enough that you don't feel like you have to go over all the time or you can't have what you want. It's nice to have it be little enough that it takes time to save up for big purchases and you can have time to think about what you want and if you really do want or need it.

One year, I waited to buy my *Blendtec* because I wanted to make sure I would really use it. It has been three or four years now, and I still love it and use it regularly, so I don't regret the purchase one bit. This is what I hope to help you do; remove some of the guilt that overspending can cause. Guilt is an awful part of bipolar depression, so removing any of it can make a big difference.

Budget

A basic budget is essential. This can be a good thing to do in either or both phases, to help you remember where your money needs to go. Try to whittle away at the base budget and bring the base amount of income that you need to survive to the smallest amount possible. This can be done in a variety of ways. Cut nonessential items, conserve resources, and sometimes you may need to shop around.

If you carry any credit card debt, I would suggest paying it down as quickly as possible and once it's gone, pay it off monthly. It is easy to say you will pay it later and have it build up without any consequences being considered. If you need to, cut up the credit cards and deal with debit cards and cash only. Another route that I have considered, is putting my budget on a reloadable credit card so that when it's gone, it's gone and I can't overspend with it.

Safety nets are essential in the budget. My solution to this, and one I would highly suggest is something we call "personal money" in our house. We allot an amount that is currently 6% of our monthly income each. You can lower or raise this to a reasonable amount for your family. Beyond our base needs, almost everything comes from this, gifts, clothes, extra food (like eating out) and entertainment. It does take some prioritizing, but that helps ensure that they are truly things that you want and not an impulse decision.

Roadblocks

These are designed to rein in spending and help you to be the most successful you can be without sabotaging yourself or your dreams. I find that where I like to start is by shopping at home with wish lists. Sometimes just putting something on a wish list can be satisfying enough. Also, this allows you to have a few things that you may want in mind when people ask you for gift suggestions. It gives you time to think about whether you really want something without losing where it was or forgetting you wanted it, if that is something that causes you to worry.

I like to discuss potential purchases with my spouse or a trusted friend or family member. They can often see things a little more clearly, and they know what your long-term goals are. They can help you decide if your wanted purchase fits within those guidelines. It is helpful to talk through the purchase from different angles and with varying investments in mind that may have to wait.

I try to plan for future wants by having savings within my personal money. This allows me to set aside money and have another roadblock between spending everything I have. The personal money has been the biggest block because I hate going into debt to our family and I don't do it very often. I don't like feeling like I'm taking things away from the family that I love. Extra blocks, where I have to think through decisions, is the key during hypomanic phases. The problem is that I don't think at all, not that I have completely forgotten my long-term goals. When I stop to think, I can often talk through things rationally and these steps can help you to do the same.

One of the best tools is to delay gratification, especially through a cycle or two. If you still want something during a depression that you wanted in hypomania and vice versa, it may be a true desire. I find that if I purchase something during depression, then it is normally something I really need, because I hate purchasing things when I'm depressed.

Personal Money

Start by picking a reasonable percentage of your income that you can afford to spare and that still allows for savings with the residual income. We started this number at 20%, and it was way too high. We didn't save, and we blew our extra money. I have a lot more regrets from the 20% income number than the 6%.

Personal money, when successful, should cover everything beyond the necessities needed to survive. This should include everything except shampoo, soaps, toilet paper, basic bills, and housing. This may mean that you need the percentage to be slightly higher to get this covered.

The best part of personal money is that there is no judgment ideally. You should still be discussing it with a loved one, but you are the end-all decision maker. As long as you stick within that amount, you can spend it however you want. This takes a lot of the fighting out of money situations and allows individuals to spend toward their varying desires and interests. Everything shouldn't be a fight, and you should be able to make the small personal money purchases without discussing them overly much. I do always discuss them with myself though!

A running list of purchases and running checkbook of debits and credits is also essential. This is not somewhere you want to be dishonest or sloppy. When I find myself sliding and not wanting to discuss purchases with my spouse, I know that I need to rein myself in or pull back and reevaluate where I am. I find that when I start lying or wanting to lie, I'm in a very risky place and I need to take that leap of fear and trust to reconnect with my spouse. He has my best interest at heart and is always looking out for me. For bipolar people, it is important to find someone you can trust who can help you gauge reality and keep you on track.

Questions to Ask Before a Purchase

- Is this in line with my long-term goals?
- How will I use this?
- How long will it be useful?
- How long have I wanted it?
- Am I hypomanic or manic?
- Do I have the personal money saved to buy this?

14

Managing Expectations: Part 1

Love Yourself

There are many ways to love yourself, and all but selfish, narcissistic love, is valid and helpful. Something we often tend to forget is that you have to love yourself first before you can share that love with others, and the better you love yourself, the better you can love others. I have a few strategies that I use to increasingly show love for myself and make sure that I am engaging in proper self-care.

Something we often tend to forget is that you have to love yourself first before you can share that love with others, and the better you love yourself, the better you can love others.

One of my favorites, I found back in 2012, from a brilliant blog post titled *Drops of Awesome*. The idea behind this technique is that if you do one thing (and give yourself credit), you might be able to do another thing, but at that moment, you are a person who puts away the dishes or folds the clothes, etc. You don't worry about what you have done in the past or will do in the future. You also let Christ make up the difference. Now whether you are religious or not, this technique can make a huge difference in your life. I used it as a gratitude journal. I would go throughout my day saying, "Drops of awesome" after doing small or large tasks. Then I would record them in my journal before going to bed and be grateful for all that I *was* able to accomplish. I found that this helped improve my depression and hypomania.

Another technique is to count your blessings, either as you fall asleep, or as you go about your day. This can help you feel loved and start to see your own worth and love yourself. I want to mention here that your worth is not based on your actions. You are of infinite worth and your worth doesn't decrease if you can't get out of bed and take a shower. Your worth also doesn't naturally increase based on your ability to accomplish things. This is no longer my definition of success. I'm still working on it, but my new definition of success is based on relationships and my journey toward my Savior. Success isn't how much money we acquire or how good we are at our job.

Another good thing to remember is that nothing lasts forever. This can be a huge relief for the bipolar individual. When in the depths of depression, or an awful irritable phase, it can feel like it will never end. This tends to be around the time when things get better. I often hit a low and have to endure it before things get better. There is a point when no strategy works, and you're just tired and have no more motivation or willpower. Just know that during this time your support system both physical and spiritual are carrying you. You're not as alone as you feel and this is a time to ask whatever Higher Power you believe in if you are loved and of worth. You can feel the truth of this, and it can be a great comfort.

I also want to mention that it is okay to lean on others and also, to cry. Sometimes in my depression, I even watch a sad movie because I can't cry and I know I need to. It often does the trick and I feel better afterward.

Phases: Depression

During the depression phase, it is important to be kind to yourself and delegate tasks often and early. When I know I'm fully in a depression, I will evaluate my obligations and responsibilities and eliminate everything that isn't absolutely essential. I ask my mom for help with school volunteer hours, and we split them. I ask to be released from my church responsibilities that are too overwhelming and keep me from attending if I can't fulfill them. I decrease shopping to the minimum and ask my husband to come with me. On this one, I recommend using pick-up options at your store if they have them. This offers the option of picking up your groceries curbside and can decrease time and anxiety. The point is to get rid of everything nonessential that will cause you stress while you still feel good enough to do so.

Remember that one small thing each day can be huge and is a valid accomplishment. Sometimes I just need to do one load of dishes or laundry, and that's all I require of myself that day to let it be a good day. Sometimes the accomplishment is taking my blanket and going from my bed to the couch for a change of scenery. Decide what it will be for you in the morning and congratulate yourself when you accomplish it that evening.

A companion to this would be praising the little things. This goes along with "drops of awesome." Small tasks, repeated consistently, create big accomplishments. Don't let go of your long-term goals, just manage your expectations. If you are writing a book, spend five minutes on it, instead of an hour or two, like you might do when you feel up to it. Keep the habit and keep the things that bring you joy.

Try hard! You can fight this, especially in the beginning. Although it is important to take out the things you can't do, it is also important to keep the reasonable ones. I find that accomplishments, and feeling valued and appreciated, are essential to helping me get out of the depressive state. I need to feel worthy and useful to want to fight for myself and continue going even when I feel like giving up.

Phases: Mania

The mania is such a different animal from the depression, but at the same time, you still need to care for yourself and manage expectations. You must know that even if you don't feel tired you still have limits and they need to be enforced (by you!) You can't rely on someone else to hold you back, because you probably won't listen to them, or you may start feeling resentment toward them. I limit myself to one big activity a week outside the home.

If I find myself taking on too many things, I rein it in and remove extra obligations. I also enforce nonnegotiable down days. These are days where I stay home and care for things at home and relax with no major obligations.

It is important to be gentle with yourself. You can't improve everything at one time. Take one tool at a time that you want to change and work to implement it for a month. If you don't like it then try something else. Not everything will work for everyone, but you will find things that improve your quality of life and can help you find balance and peace. It may not look like what you consider a normal lifestyle, but you have to do what works for you. If someone else is judging you for your lifestyle, remember to stick to what works for you. You know your needs best.

Done is Key

This comes from the popular idea that *done is better than perfect*. Work to accomplish your long-term goals whenever you can. I find that my early stages of depression and hypomania and anything that feels "middle ground normal" are the best times to get things done. You want to utilize opportunities to move forward with your long-term goals. However, remember to keep it within reason. Burnout can happen fast in any phase.

The deep depression is a time to heal and not worry too much if you aren't able to keep up with your goals and habits. It always ends, and you will be able to try again and be a little more successful the next time. The obsession and procrastination that come from worry and anxiety aren't a good mix for accomplishing your goals.

It is okay to settle for good. Sometimes it is honestly the best you can do. I have had years where my grades were A's, and I hated it and regretted it because of the pain it caused me. There were other periods when I got B's and C's, it was the best I could do at the time, and I was healthy. My freshman year of high school I got A's, but I was trying to be perfect and white-knuckle it. It was extremely hard on me physically and mentally. I remember writing a three-page paper at home with both my parents trying to help me late into the night because I was depressed and deleting everything as I went, because it sounded awful and I beat myself up mentally the whole way.

There was also a time when I was feeling great and very organized, right after I was married. I was able to get a 3.82 GPA my sophomore year of college and all was well. I didn't crash afterward, and I managed my time and rest well.

Sometimes settling for done is the best self-care you can give. It isn't worth perfecting things over and over again if what you really need is sleep and rest. Learning to do your best with where you're at is vital. This takes practice and isn't an exact science, as it changes each day. This will be one of the greatest things you do for yourself and is a good place to start with an experiment in learning to love yourself.

15

Managing Expectations: Part 2

Tell People

One of my biggest fears after my diagnosis, and before I fully accepted it, was telling people that I have bipolar. I denied it for so long because I was afraid of what their reactions might be or that it somehow made it more real. Now I work hard to tell people who may be affected by my symptoms ahead of time what they need to know. This can be people who are relying on you, knowing that you may need to lean on them during certain times. Whatever it is, it is personal to you, but the key is to set up support systems for your success so that you won't have to tell people once you desperately need their help.

I also let my friends, that I meet while I'm hypomanic, know that I may disappear from social media and stop calling suddenly. I want them to know beforehand that I'm okay and that my depression is normal and I can manage it, and I will be back to being friends with them as soon as I can.

Share your diagnosis any time you feel you need to. I now drop it in casual conversation, and sometimes people raise their eyebrows, but more often than not, I get positive responses. Almost everyone knows someone who has bipolar, or they have bipolar themselves. Many people praise me for my openness and courage. I can be a voice for those who aren't ready to lay it all on the table yet.

Moderation

Keep in mind that you don't have to tell every person you meet about your diagnosis. You can tell people if and when you are comfortable, and you may want to keep it to yourself at times, either for your benefit, or the benefit of those around you. Also, this is a good time to remind you that it is never a good idea to share someone else's diagnosis with others. It is their news to tell. There are a few exceptions here. I don't care if people tell others about my diagnosis if I don't know them and they don't know me, but that person is helping provide support. An example of this, is my mom sharing with one of her friends to help them with their mentally ill children or friends.

It is also okay to say that you are sick with no further explanation. Sometimes it is better to leave information out than overload someone with information they just don't need. Just because I'm mentally sick rather than physically sick doesn't make it any less valid. Sometimes the reason I want to explain is because of anxiety and pressured speech. I feel obligated to give someone an explanation because I don't believe that it is valid for me to say I'm sick and just stay home. The main reason behind this is most likely social, but I hope as I continue to push my comfort zone, I will eventually become more comfortable with my illness and treat it as valid, because it is.

Accept Help

The people who love you are there and want to help you. They need your help to know how. Those who have no experience with mental illness, but love you, just need you to say the word, and they will be right there. Most people who have bipolar, help others when they feel good. It's okay to accept help when you need it. It isn't admitting defeat, and it's hard, but it is worth it to connect with the people who love you.

Sometimes you really need that help. It seems to be easier for me to accept if it comes from family, and if that is an option for you, it is a great one. You can create your own family from friends if you don't have close family. Church family can be a great help if you are religious. Let them bring you meals if you really need them. Let them help you with some overwhelming house cleaning tasks. Sometimes you can do it all, but you have to be willing to accept your limits and take care of yourself when you can't, for your family and yourself.

Build a support system of people who you trust and can be really honest with. This can be a best friend, siblings, in-laws, and parents. It can be anything that works for your own normal. Work to become more comfortable with your support group by sharing what life looks like for you and asking for help when you need it by letting them in. Being open can go a long way to helping people understand. You want them to have reasonable and accurate expectations of you so they can truly help. Another good idea is just to let it out sometimes. If your friends and family can't handle your emotions, then at least you know. Anyone who can't handle your true feelings probably needs to be removed from this list. This doesn't mean you can't be friends with them, but you probably can't rely on them for support.

Boundaries

Bipolar people are easy targets for manipulation. During hypomania, I tend to be a people-pleaser because I want to be social and I don't want to deal with any conflict. I am willing to take on everything, and so I frequently say yes, not only because I want to, but because it is too uncomfortable to say no. This makes it very easy to try to help others and end up hurting myself or neglecting self-care and crashing.

Creating boundaries is a big part of self-care and keeping yourself from over-committing. Often, it is very difficult to get out of situations if others are manipulative and you haven't created boundaries. In my experience, I get so that I see someone on an almost daily basis, and if there are any manipulative situations, it's hard to get out of them. I find that creating distance to decide what boundaries are necessary is the best tactic. Pulling yourself out of a situation allows you to look at it more objectively without all the emotions and desires to see the person or help them.

Then once you have a grasp on the situation, you can decide if you can continue the relationship with some modifications and clear boundaries defined, or if you need to end the relationship altogether. Some modifications could be limiting your time together. It could also be saying no to anything that is adding too much to your plate. There are many scenarios, but you simply have to make sure you are prioritizing yourself and your family over the other person.

When protecting your sanity, you can't be totally unselfish. Although it is easy to be overly selfish and lack humility when you're hypomanic, it is important to remember that throwing selfishness completely out the window isn't the answer. Prioritizing appropriately is a good answer to this problem. For your sake and your family's sake, it's important to prioritize family over friends. If you need to think of it as prioritizing your family over strangers or friends, that will make it less selfish. Just make sure that you do it.

I have lost months and months trying to please people who weren't even good friends. They were just using me because I would do whatever they wanted. As soon as I was depressed or if I stuck up for myself, they disappeared.

16

Managing Responses

With Love

This brings us to managing how other people react to having bipolar or mental illnesses in general. Sometimes you have to let things just roll off your back. So many people, who have never been touched by mental illness, have incorrect ideas of how it really is. These may be the people who say "snap out of it" or "you're making it up" or "it's just an excuse." Although these are hard to take, there is often no point in wasting your time trying to correct them. It is just ignorance, and their opinions may change when they experience it for themselves or with a close family member. It is not always your responsibility to end the stigma with each individual.

When the misconception is harmful, I do think it is worth correcting though. I once had someone tell me that their loved one was having these problems, what looked like bipolar to me, because of past sins in their lives that they needed to resolve. This is just plain wrong. Even in the bible, Jesus states that neither the man or the parent sinned with the man who was blind. I know mistakes, and their consequences can make our lives harder, but they don't cause mental illness.

Try to listen and absorb the care from well-meaning individuals while letting the ignorance go. So many people that love you won't know how to handle your diagnosis and before they learn more about it, they may say things that are hurtful. I was speaking with my mom recently, and used the word crazy. She laughed a little and said that I used to get angry when she used that word. I'm sure it was a trigger for me around my diagnosis. Now it is not so much of an issue, but I wish I could have let it go back then, since people use that word without meaning it in a harmful way, but simply part of our usual conversation.

With Confidence

Bipolar people are more likely to be victimized by violence and abuse than the general population. You have to learn to stand up for yourself because sometimes no one else will be there to do so. People can be cruel with their ignorance, and sometimes you need to stand up to the bullying and correct their misconceptions.

Be an advocate for those who can't be, because you are either there now, or you have been there before. I remember what it was like to be in denial and afraid of telling anyone what was really going on. I didn't believe my diagnosis was real, so why would I tell anyone a truth I didn't even believe? However, watching people bravely live their truth has given me the courage to open up and be who I am. It is such a relief to be myself and a much more enjoyable experience. Now I can stand up and be a voice for those who aren't ready yet. I'm also able to be a silent support system for them as well. There have been those who have private messaged me with what was going on after seeing my blog posts. If I hadn't been open about it, and if no one else was, how would they get the support they needed?

Once you're ready, help end the stigma, and bravely share your truth. Help people understand your new normal and that it is understandable, valid, and okay. This helps you immensely, but it also helps others who can't do that quite yet, to see your bravery.

Be bold! Sometimes this one can be a little fun. My husband recently shared with me that he loves watching the faces of our friends, family, and acquaintances every time I drop info about my mental health. I use terms in casual conversation like depression, mania, bipolar, etc. I just go with it, and most people do too. I don't think I have had a horrible reaction yet, at least not to my face. It is kind of fun too, to shock people a bit and see their reactions. It should be easy to mention, just like it is to mention physical illnesses like the flu and having knee surgery. It is a different type of illness of course, but why does it have to make people uncomfortable. I know handicaps make a lot of people uncomfortable as well. There is definitely work that can be done there, but we can only really work with what we know.

With Teaching

When people don't understand but are willing to try, they need to be educated. Share your experiences once you feel comfortable. Although it may seem simple and normal for you, it is a totally new world for those who are learning about it for the first time.

It is easy to see the differences between mental illness and everyday experiences by those who don't deal with mental illnesses. I prefer to focus on the similarities. Bipolar hypomania is extreme for the individual, however, the emotions and actions aren't always outside the realms of normal except for that person. There are some points along the bipolar spectrum that other people can relate to. Maybe it's anxiety which people can relate to, and then extrapolate how it might be if it were more extreme. The same can be said for irritability, depression, etc.

One of the easiest explanations for many people to understand, is to explain hypomania as teenage behaviors. That is why it can be so hard for parents of bipolar teens to distinguish between what is the bipolar and what is classic teen behavior. I'm 27, and I act like a reckless teenager a few weeks out of the year. It is scary and at times, afterward, hilarious!

Depression can be understood with people's situational depression.

71

Depression from crisis and from losing loved ones, can be similar to bipolar depression. Everyone has their own experiences, but it helps to build community to find things in common rather than pointing out our differences and distancing ourselves from one another.

Reactions

I have gotten all kinds of reactions from people when I tell them I have bipolar or explain what it is like to be me. I'm sure other people have gotten worse reactions than I have. I have actually received extremely positive responses most of my life. Especially since I accepted myself and gained greater confidence.

Some people's reactions are mute. Many are curious and ask me questions because they have a family member or friend they think may have bipolar. These people are the most fun, and it's easiest to deal with their reactions. They are simply interested, and it is fun to share and open up to them.

Many are very supportive because the illness has touched them in one way or another, either through a family member, friend, or themselves. They get it, and they are happy to help as best they can and listen when necessary. They also know when to help and push you a bit to be your best.

The hard ones to deal with are people who believe mental illness comes from sin as a punishment, or think it is all in your head. They don't understand why you need special circumstances and why things could be so hard when nothing is visibly wrong.

17

Conclusion

Thank you so much for reading my book, and congratulations on making it all the way through!

I have loved writing this book. If it helps even one person, it will have been worth it. It has been an incredible experience already, and I can't wait to see where it goes. Thank you to everyone who has supported me through this process. I love you for it.

I'm no longer afraid to be me. I'm okay with losing a few friends for what I can gain from being open and true to myself. I love taking a holistic approach to creating my own normal, and I can't wait to hear how you successfully create your own normal as well. Please don't hesitate to let me know your experiences with the book. I would love to hear from you. My email is balancingmybipolar@gmail.com.

Also, if you find any errors or potential errors in the book, please let me know by using the email above as well. I want my book to be as good as it can be, and I know reading books with mistakes can take you out of the story, and the experience.

Ever since I began struggling with bipolar, I have told myself that this would all be worth it if I were able to help someone else with their own experience. This is a big part of why I wrote this book, and I hope it can assist you in your own life or in understanding a loved one.

I refuse to fit in a box, just to help other people feel better. I will no longer be embarrassed or silent. I'm here to help people and to show

how great life can be, regardless of your challenges!

Acknowledgements

I want to give a huge thank you to my accountability partners Glenda Gabriel and Jen Truong. They helped me keep my perspective, pushed me to be better, and helped me stay on track.

I am so grateful for my beta readers, including my mom, who is one of my greatest champions.

A huge thank you to my editor, Qat Wanders, who worked so well with me and helped smooth my rough draft into a finished product.

Also, I couldn't have done this without my husband, who supports me through all my endeavors. He watched my girls frequently so I could work, and helped me sleep in and take naps when I stayed up late writing.

Thank you to all of my friends that I mention in this book. I don't say anything to hurt anyone, and you are all amazing.

Request for Reviews

Thank you so much for taking the time to read *Balancing Your Bipolar*. I have loved writing this book, and I genuinely hope that it can make a difference for you.

If you find any errors, please send me an email at balancingmybipolar@gmail.com, with the subject line error. I have worked hard to make my book error-free, but I know that I'm not perfect and I would like the experience to be the best possible.

If you enjoyed the book, I would love to hear your honest reviews on Amazon or any other platform you use. I know these reviews are important to help other readers find my book and I would truly appreciate your support.

About the Author

Blythe Edwards is a first-time author, mom, wife, and friend. She lives in Southern Utah County, Utah with her family, dogs, chickens, and garden. Ever since her diagnosis, she has hoped to be able to reach out to others and help them have hope and improve their lives through what she has learned. Her dream has come true in the form of this book.

You can connect with me on:
- https://twitter.com/BMEdwardsAuthor
- https://www.facebook.com/balancingmybipolar
- https://www.instagram.com/balancingmybipolar

Subscribe to my newsletter:
- http://eepurl.com/c_wmF5

Made in the USA
Monee, IL
01 December 2019